People of the Bible

The Bible through stories and pictures

Moses and the Plagues

Copyright © in this format Belitha Press Ltd., 1985

Text copyright © Catherine Storr 1985

Illustrations copyright © Jim Russell 1985

Art Director: Treld Bicknell

First published in the United States of America 1985
by Raintree Publishers Limited Partnership
310 West Wisconsin Avenue, Milwaukee, Wisconsin 53203
in association with Belitha Press Ltd., London.

Conceived, designed and produced by Belitha Press Ltd.,
2 Beresford Terrace, London N5 2DH

ISBN 0-8172-1999-4 (U.S.A.)

Library of Congress Cataloging in Publication Data

Storr, Catherine.
    Moses and the plagues.

    (People of the Bible)
    Summary: God sends plagues upon the Egyptians for
not allowing the Israelites to leave Egypt under the
leadership of Moses.
    1. Moses (Biblical leader)—Juvenile literature.
2. Plagues of Egypt—Juvenile literature. [1. Moses
(Biblical leader) 2. Plagues of Egypt. 3. Bible
stories—O.T.] I. Title. II. Series.
BS580.M6S755   1984   222'.1209505   84-18077

ISBN 0-8172-1999-4

First published in Great Britain in paperback 1985
by Methuen Children's Books Ltd.,
11 New Fetter Lane, London EC4P 4EE

7 8 9 10 11 12 13   98 97 96 95 94 93 92 91 90

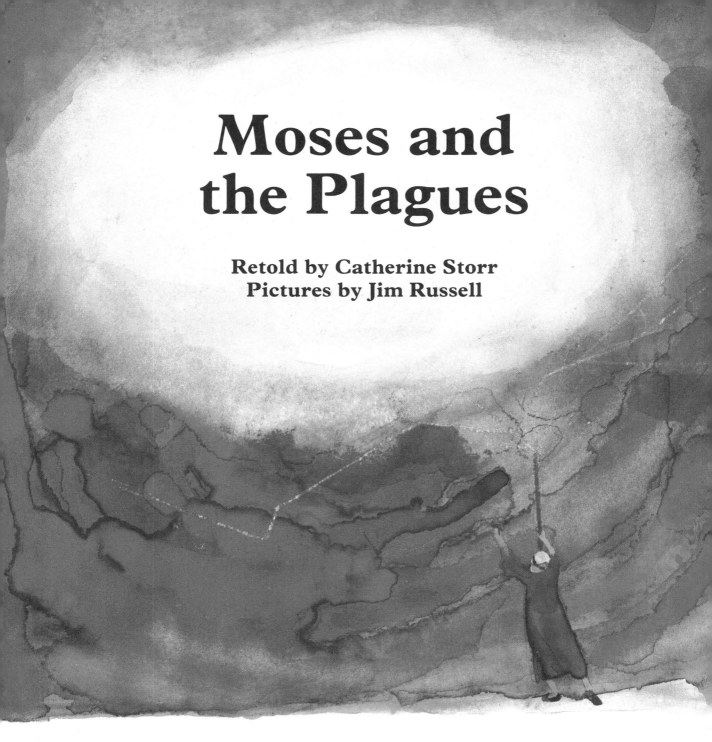

Moses and the Plagues

Retold by Catherine Storr
Pictures by Jim Russell

Raintree Publishers
Milwaukee
Belitha Press Limited • London

God had told Moses and Aaron to go to Egypt. They were to stand before Pharaoh and to ask him to let the Children of Israel go.

But Pharaoh said, "You are making the
Israelites lazy." He ordered the taskmasters to
stop giving them straw for making bricks. But
they were still supposed to make as many
bricks as before. When they could not, the
Israelite foremen were beaten.

The foremen sent to Pharaoh, asking, "Why do you treat us like this? We cannot make bricks without straw." Pharaoh replied, "You are too lazy."

Then the Israelites blamed Moses and Aaron. "It is your fault that Pharaoh is angry with us," they said. "He has told his servants to kill us."

Moses said to God, "Why did you send me to bring trouble on your people."

God said, "Go again to Pharaoh."

But Moses said, "He will not take any notice of what I say."

God said, "I will make him listen. But I shall also harden his heart. Then I shall show many wonders in the land, so that Pharaoh will know that I am the Lord.

"Pharaoh will ask you to show him a miracle. Tell your brother, Aaron, to cast down his rod before Pharaoh. It will become a serpent."

Moses did as God said. When Pharaoh saw it, he made his magicians cast down *their* rods. They all became serpents, and Aaron's serpent swallowed all the other serpents.

11

But Pharaoh's heart was hardened, and he would not let the people go.

God told Aaron to strike the waters of the river with his rod. When Aaron did, the waters turned to blood. The fish died, and the river stank, and no one could drink.

Pharaoh would not listen to anyone. He went into his house, and his heart was hard.

God said to Moses, "Tell Aaron to stretch his hand over the streams and the river and the ponds. Then the land of Egypt will be covered with frogs."

Aaron stretched out his hand, and frogs came out of the water and covered the land. Pharaoh's magicians did the same.

Then Pharaoh sent for Moses and Aaron and said, "Ask your god to take away these frogs, and I will let your people go."

But when the frogs had gone, Pharaoh
hardened his heart and would not let the
Children of Israel go.

God told Aaron to stretch out his rod and to
smite the dust of the land. When Aaron smote
the dust, it turned into lice. Every man and
woman and animal in Egypt was covered with
lice.

Pharaoh's magicians tried to do the same thing, but they could not. They said to Pharaoh, "This is the anger of God."
But Pharaoh's heart was still hard.

God said to Moses, "Get up early in the morning and meet Pharaoh as he goes to bathe. Say to him, 'The Lord tells you to let his people go. If you will not, he will send swarms of flies into your houses. Then you will know that he is the Lord of Heaven and Earth.'"

The next day the Egyptian houses were full of flies. Pharaoh said to Moses, "Go and sacrifice to your Lord, and ask him to take away these flies. Then I will let the people go."

Moses and Aaron went out into the wilderness and pleaded with God to take away the flies. He did.

But Pharaoh hardened his heart again.

Then God said to Moses, "Tell Pharaoh that I am the Lord God of the Hebrews. If he will not let them leave Egypt, I will bring disease to all his cattle." Pharaoh saw that his cattle died, but the cattle of the Israelites were well and healthy.

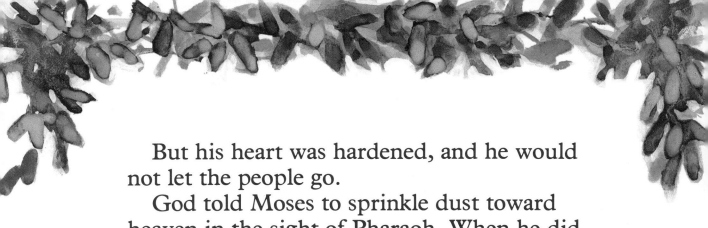

But his heart was hardened, and he would not let the people go.

God told Moses to sprinkle dust toward heaven in the sight of Pharaoh. When he did this, all the Egyptians were covered with boils and sores.

Pharaoh's magicians could not stand before Pharaoh because of their sores.

But God hardened Pharaoh's heart, and he would not listen to their entreaties that he should let the Israelites go.

God told Moses to stretch out his hand toward the heavens.

Then there fell a terrible hail, breaking trees and plants, and bruising men and beasts.

Pharaoh said to Moses and Aaron, "I have sinned. Your Lord is good. Ask him to stop this hail, and I will let the people go."

The Lord said to Moses, "I have hardened Pharaoh's heart so that I may show him my greatness. Tell him that I shall bring more locusts than he or his father or his father's father have ever seen." Pharaoh's servants said to Pharaoh, "Let these people go, or all Egypt will be destroyed."

Pharaoh said to Moses, "You and your children can go, but the men must stay here." Moses would not agree. So the locusts came in their millions and ate up every leaf in the land of Egypt.

Pharaoh said to Moses, "I have sinned against the Lord your God and against you. Take away the locusts." Moses entreated God, and God sent a mighty wind which blew away the locusts.

But because Pharaoh's heart was hardened again, God sent a darkness over the land, so thick that it could be felt. Pharaoh said he would let all the Israelites go. But when the darkness was taken away, God hardened his heart once more.

28

Then God said, "I will bring one more plague to Egypt. Then Pharaoh will not just let you go, he will thrust you out. I am going to kill the first-born child of every Egyptian. The eldest son of Pharaoh and of his servants and of his animals will die. But I will not kill the sons of Israel.

"In every house of my people a lamb must be killed. The people of the house must eat the lamb roasted, and they must smear its blood on the sideposts and the lintels of the door.

Then I will know that it is an Israelite house and will not strike. Keep this rite as the Feast of the Passover."

After the Passover, Pharaoh sent for Moses and Aaron. He said "Take what you want and go at once out of Egypt!"

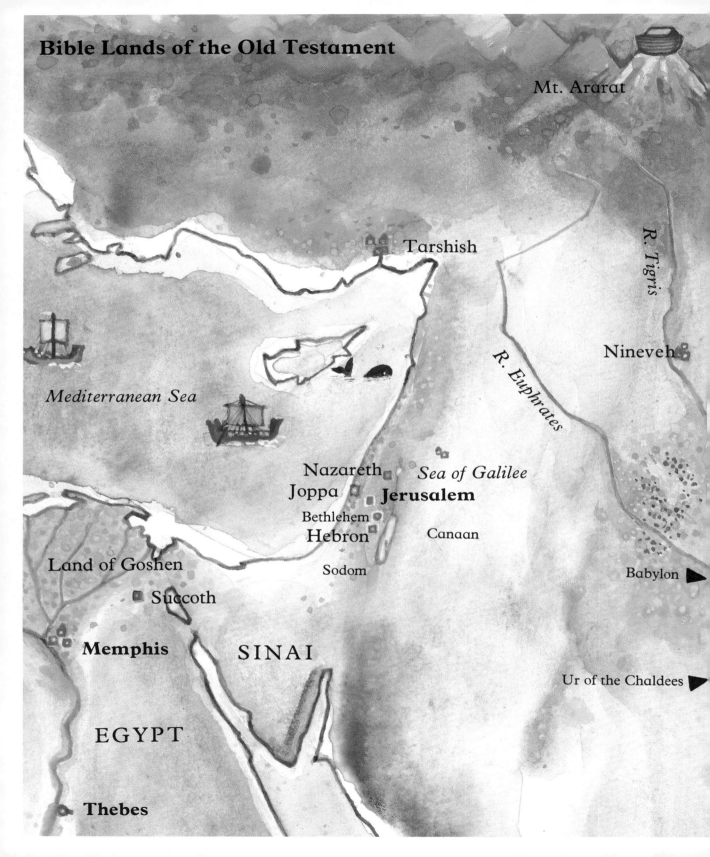

Bible Lands of the Old Testament

Mt. Ararat

Tarshish

R. Tigris

Nineveh

R. Euphrates

Mediterranean Sea

Nazareth   *Sea of Galilee*

Joppa   **Jerusalem**

Bethlehem

Hebron   Canaan

Sodom

Land of Goshen   Babylon ▶

Succoth

Ur of the Chaldees ▶

Memphis   S I N A I

Thebes   E G Y P T